51 shades of Business

Marketing Introduction

The Marketing Big Picture for Total Beginners!

Koz Khosravani

Table of Contents

51 shades of Business marketing Introduction

The Marketing Big Picture for Total Beginners!

Welcome to my mini book – the 51 shades of business marketing. This book is definitely not an in-depth look at various online marketing methods (calling them shades here) such as search engine optimization (SEO) or pay per click advertising (PPC). Instead, it's a reminder book for beginners on what methods or shades exists for online marketing so then the readers can do more online research about it. So why am I writing this book? Mainly because people are only familiar with few just a few shades such as SEO, PPC, social media marketing (mainly Facebook) and that is about it. My hope is that after glancing at my mini book, you would know what the possibilities are and then do more research on those possibilities.

In general, I divide the process of online success into a few categories (view the big picture below):

- Business Foundation

- Online Presence

- Business Reputation & Branding

- Success Education

- Conversion Success

- Online Marketing

- Offline Marketing

- Mobile Marketing

- Sales Support Tools & Automation

Ok, after you absorbed the image shown below, get started. If you wanted to view this image with large size (highly recommended to download as my gift to you), visit:

http://www.DigiFusionMedia.com/bigpicture.jpg

Under each of those categories there are many shades of marketing. For example, under the category of "Offline Marketing", you will find shades of TV ads, Radio ads, Direct Mail and so forth. So please choose an area that you are interested in (e.g. Online Presence) and then under each category choose your favorite shade (e.g. squeeze page) and learn about it further.... Ready, set, GO!

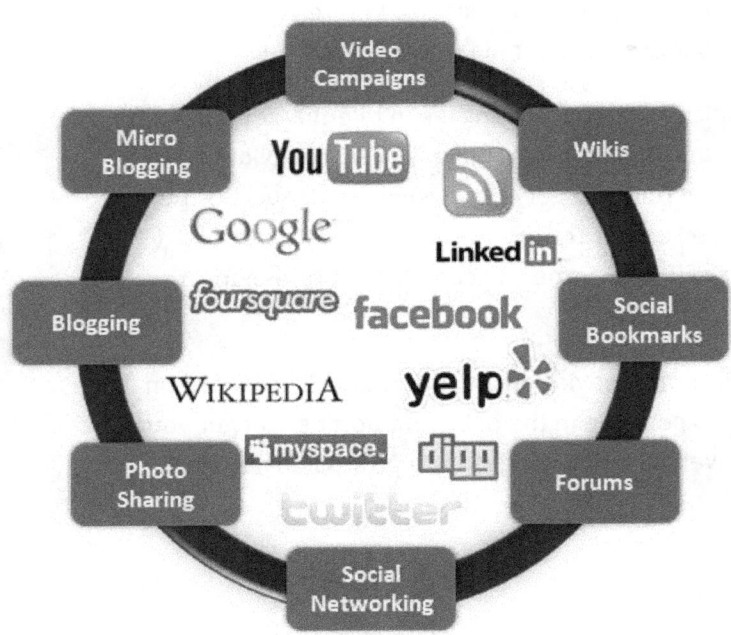

Disclosure and Legal Notice

Ready? Not so fast! Please note that we cannot offer legal, tax or similar professional advice. We are **NOT** lawyers or tax professionals. The content of this book is educational in nature. It is written based on years of our experience in business marketing.

But you MUST meet your attorney, CPA and other relevant professionals to get professional advice before you start a business or to implement our ideas in your business.

As an example, if you want to engage in tele-marketing, email marketing or direct marketing, you MUST follow the law and certain rules. So get educated in places such as the website of the Federal Trade Commission and definitely get the blessing of your attorney, tax and other professional to implement stuff.

Again, we only offer advice on an educational level based on our years of experience in the field. But don't endanger your finances or well-being by not getting a professional advice. Just do it!

Business Foundation

Passion, Goals & Vision

Well, no business would make it big unless you have passion for what you do, have proper goals and have a vision for the future of your business. Stop here if you don't have these MUST ingredients!

Business Planning

You need a business plan. Or maybe not! Don't avoid starting a business just because you don't have an official, fancy, business plan. And yet, there are things in the plan that are a must for your business success. These include knowing your market, competition, audience, products and services (see below).

Services Analysis

You must analyze the services that you offer in your venture. Are they needed in the market? Are your services unique? Do you offer good prices for your services? Seriously, don't fall in love with your business services. Have a clear look at them and see if you are adding anything of value for your prospects.

Prospect Analysis

You MUST know your prospects. You can't just try to market your products and services to everyone (even if everyone can use it). By focusing on a niche group of prospects, you can lower your marketing cost so you can reach out to them. For something as simple as your online presence, a design of your website will differ if your audiences are conservative accountants vs. rock bands! How can you have a right design for the site if you don't know your precise, exact, niche audience?

Business Finance

Listen, you can have all the passion in the world for your business but I know too many startups that went belly up since they did not have money to continue after the first few months. Yes, many firms start with very little money, but do your homework and see if you can generate income real fast if you have no money for operations, marketing, etc.

Legal Issues

I cannot give you legal advice here since I am not an attorney. And yet, all I know is that if you open a corporation or LLC, you can in most cases reduce your personal liability to minimum. If you can't afford an attorney to start a LLC for you, at least hire cheap but quality alternative services such as legalzoom.com or similar firms. For just a few hundred dollars you can buy yourself peace of mind. Enough said. Visit legalzoom.com and you will know what to do. But nothing replaces an experienced attorney. They are worth it and can save you lots of headache not to mention legal challenges.

Accounting

As a small startup you might not need a fancy CPA or accounting firm representing you. But at minimum, use

Google search to find information out there about basic bookkeeping, accounting, etc. Better yet, invest a little money in business accounting software like business turbo tax, etc. A good accountant (like a lawyer) can save you a lot if you can afford them though. So get one to help you with your business. We cannot give you legal or tax advice.

Entrepreneurial Psychology

I hate to say this. You NEED to have an entrepreneurial mindset. Too many things will go wrong in a business or business startup and you can't just give up or be risk averse! You have to be able to take educate risks; to go against all odds; to constantly educate yourself about your business, market, competition, etc. I simply don't believe some people are made to be entrepreneurs. So think hard about this area. Do you have what it takes?

Promotional Graphics

You need to have a great logo, graphics for your site, graphics for your business card, etc. Don't go craze spending thousands of dollars hiring an expensive graphic artist. I simply use the services of vistaprint.com and do stuff myself. Keep your money for operating and marketing your business. Things will go wrong – save!

Business Stationary

In all honesty in many new online businesses, we don't even need any fancy stationary, letters, envelopes, etc. Almost everything is done online. And yet for when you need it, order some from vistaprint.com or similar online services. Cheap and high quality... By the way, I don't work for Vistaprint nor make any money sending you to them! I just like their simple yet effective do-it-yourself services!

Online Presence

Koz Khosravani
former Harvard & UCLA lecturer
Donald Trump's Marketing Guru

Websites

Invest in having a great site. Don't hire web designers to design a website for you! Instead, hire internet marketers to do it for you. Web designers will make you and your cousin happy. Internet marketers will try to design for your niche audience so you make money. They know about design that is search engine friendly and much more! Invest some money here and own a professional site that makes a good first impression.

E-Commerce Sites

This is the same as a website and yet you have additional features such as a shopping cart, payment processing capability, online security capability, etc. If you sell products online (instead of just offering services) you will definitely need an ecommerce site! Know in advance if you need a website or e-Commerce site!

Or your business at minimum you need presence on Facebook, twitter, LinkedIn and YouTube, followed by Instagram, Pinterest, etc. for product visual marketing.

Blogs

Blog is a journal and with it you can get followers which can lead to customers! You can have an internal blog in your website or can create an independent blog using blogger.com and Wordpress. Both are free, powerful, and effective and can get you some good search engine exposure!

Landing Pages

What is a landing page? It is a page in your site for marketing purposes (mostly but not always). Imagine your sell fruits. You have pages in your site for apples, oranges, grapes, etc. When you advertise somewhere to sell oranges for example, why should you send the prospects to your site home page? Instead send them directly to the page in your site that covers oranges! That page is called a landing page....

Squeeze Pages

A landing page is a page in your website. A squeeze page is an independent site that only has 1 page (not part of your website). Sometimes you should not confuse people with lots of information shown in your main site. If you know through research and marketing they want oranges, just send them to a 1 page independent site that sells oranges! Simple!

Micro blog

Micro blog is a blog that restricts you to certain number of characters (we are talking about the length of your message). Twitter is a good example of a micro-blog.

Online Content

Your online success in many ways will depend on creating great online content about your products, services and even your industry. Why? Search engines love good online content (higher ranks for you) and humans (your prospects) love sites that are educational and offer lots of content. You become a source of authority and build credibility for your venture.

Unique Templates

Don't have money to hire someone to create a website for you? Well, there are online templates (free or cheap) that allow you to build your online presence within minutes. For example, if you are into real estate, there are templates on Godaddy.com that allows you to have a cool looking real estate site within minutes! It won't be customized or unique but will do the job if you have neither money nor time!

SSL & HTTPS Security

If you sell stuff online you want people to trust you to use their credit cards online. You must have SSL security on your site so when the customers write their name, address, credit card info, etc the site address changes from http://www.yoursite.com to https://www.yoursite.com. That "S" after http shows that the site is secure…. Ask your web developer or hosting company about it…. Lack of this security can add to potential liabilities, my lawyer says…

Reputation & Branding

Online Brand

Your online brand will help your business. From your logo, to your website look, to your overall brand, it all helps to give you credibility online. Make sure all your online stuff has similar looks and coloring. All starbucks have similar looks, right (green)? All subways have similar look, right? This is very powerful stuff. Study about branding and implement what you can.

Offline Brand

Your offline brand is similar to online except instead of focusing on logo, website look, online graphics, etc. you will focus on tangible stuff in real world such as the brand and look on your staff shirts, stationary, marketing design on your company car, etc. Again think Starbucks, green color and how they have such powerful brand.

Online Reputation

If you have bad online reputation, you will lose business. You will lose clients. You will lose prospects... Pay attention to what is said about you, your staff and your company online. From review sites such as Yelp to Google reviews, you want as many positive reviews as possible. These days, people will Google you before they do business with you (or even to date you)! Clean up bad reputation as soon as possible and encourage happy customers to write positive reviews about your business.

Offline Reputation

Your offline reputation is as important as online reputation. If your office reception area is dirty and horrible looking, if your receptionist answers phone calls rudely, and similar things can hurt your business. I KNOW too many firms spending money to find prospects to call them and when they call, a rude (or busy) receptionist will ruin your chances!

Credibility Factor

You have competitors, right? Why should people buy from you instead of your competitors? Even when prices are the same? Well, if you have credibility, it helps. For example, I am an author of bunch of books. The fact that I am author adds credibility to my business. The fact that I am a member of better business bureau or certain association (vs. my competitors) helps my sales. The fact that my website shows my cell phone, local address and such information helps vs. a competitor who hides it all (most likely a non-local firm in another state or country). Think about your industry. What can give you an extra layer of credibility?

U.S.P. Uniqueness

Unique Selling Proposition. What makes your products or services unique? If you have a unique product then you can attract clients and customers more easily. If your competition can offer no guarantees but you can, you have uniqueness. If they don't offer refunds but you do, you have uniqueness. You get the idea. Set yourself apart from competitors. BE UNIQUE!

Reputation Shields

No one (your competitors, ex employees, jealous former boyfriend, etc) has attacked your reputation online? Great! BUT THEY WILL! It is just a matter time that someone writes bad things about your business or yourself.

You need to occupy as much online virtual real estate about yourself as possible. You should build an online reputation shield where most entries on top 3 pages of Google are your stuff, and under your control!

You need websites, many social profiles, external blogs, etc so you have control of virtual real estate about your name or your firm name. Do it now even before the potential future attack. The sooner you do the stronger your shield.

Book Authorship

Author a book about what you do and your field. It forces you to think hard about your business and industry. It gives you credibility. It might generate some extra income for you. And to be honest, it is fulfilling. You know a lot about your field. Why not help others with your knowledge....

Super-hero Factor

What is one way to guarantee success in your business? Be a super hero – helping people and your customers. Go beyond the contract and do more for your customers. Once people see you as a source of authority and know that you are not there just to sell stuff but to contribute to the well being of your customers, a super hero, you have no choice but to succeed.

Peer Group

Surround yourself with other business executives and entrepreneurs. Your peer group can do wonders for your business. Join clubs that accept only one expert per field.

Control Search Engine Entries

You can create many mini sites and external blogs to make search engine results show them instead of some unrelated stuff about you. You can change the pictures on Google top page about yourself. Take control of your brand.

Success Education

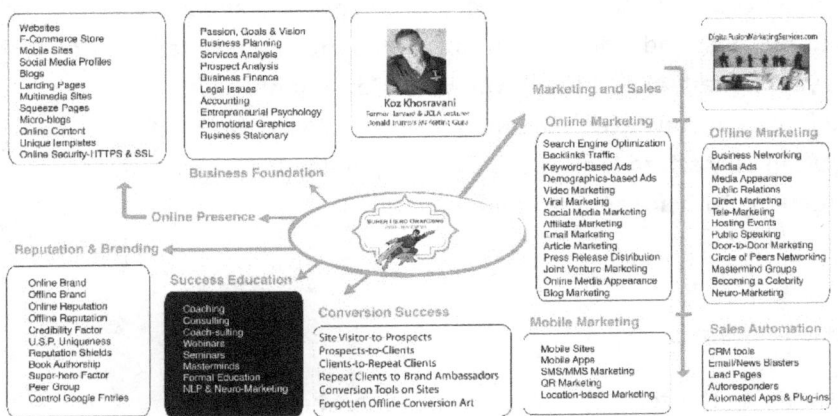

Coaching

You need a coach! Why? Because a coach can hold you accountable, motivate you, make you see the big picture even when you cannot, and by asking the right questions, point you to the right direction. There are hundreds of coaches out there. Hire the ones who would give you a free session so you can evaluate them. Walk away if they want to sell you upfront a big package for a big money without proving themselves to you first! But a good coach is worth a fortune!

Consulting

Unlike a coach, a consultant is very knowledgeable about your business and industry and can even perform many tasks on your behalf (or as a team with you). Consultants have their place if you have the money. The coaches are better if you can only afford their fee while they point you to the right direction. Both are great in general.

Coach-sulting

I just made this term up! What if someone who has both business/life/executive coaching skills also can handle many tasks and projects for you? The good news: you get the best of both worlds. The bad news: coaching advice might be tainted by the need for consultant to sell you his services! But a great Coach-sultant is a great asset on your side!

Webinars

Educate yourself all the time. The business, industry and internet world is changing rapidly. You MUST update your knowledge so taking good seminars or webinars is essential for your long term success. Webinars can be taken while you are in your home kitchen. Great convenience... No need to drive to hotel meeting rooms! But seminars have advantages over webinars!

Seminars

Seminars have similar benefits for your business and education success. The main advantage they have over webinars is that you meet your peers and potential customers face to face, and can build rapport and relationship right on spot. It can be done with webinars too but much tougher remotely.

Mastermind Groups

Find mastermind groups in your area. You will meet on a monthly (or whatever) basis with usually 5 to 20 other business entrepreneurs and executives to listen to one another, learn from one another and offer advice to one another. Great synergy to update your knowledge, plans, strategies and more!

Formal Education

Should you take courses at traditional business schools and colleges? Yes and no! It works but the time period for learning is much longer than learning on your own or online. Many college drop outs start amazing companies like Google or Microsoft. So formal education is not essential to start and operate a successful business. But it has its moments! Plus great networking opportunities with the alumni of traditional colleges...

NLP & Neuro-Marketing

A new wave of marketing based on focus on Neuro-Linguistic Programming (made famous and modified by Tony Robbins) and other marketing techniques that takes advantage of human mind, psychology and needs.

Conversion Success

Site Visitor-to-Prospects Conversion

You can have great site. You can have tons of traffic. But if you cannot convert the traffic to paying clients and customers nothing matters. That is why you take prospects through a funnel system, slowly at times! The first step is what do you do in your business and in your landing pages that turn the casual site visitor into an interested prospect (very few people buy stuff at their first exposure to your products – sometime takes 3 to 7 exposures over a period of time to build trust and relationship).

Site Prospect-to-Clients Conversion

How do you turn an interested prospect into a paying client or customer? What is it in your landing page that you offer so they trust you and buy from you? Is there powerful primary and secondary call to actions on your landing page to make the sales possible?

Site Clients-to-Repeat-Clients Conversion

The previous step made you money to pay your rent! This step makes you well off! How do you turn a paying client into a repeat client? Do you offer a variety of services or products to up-sell or cross-sell more stuff to these happy clients? And are they happy with their first purchase? They better be or this 3rd step of conversion will not work!

Site Repeat-Clients-to-Brand-Ambassadors Conversion

Ready for wealth and money? This 4th step of conversion allows you to retire to Hawaii or wherever! How do you turn your repeat clients into your brand ambassadors so they tell everyone they know about your products and services? This IS your ultimate conversion goal!

Conversion Tools

Do you have "Call To Action" sections on your landing page? Do you offer incentives to site visitors to give you their phone or email? Do you offer them something of value to download immediately? Do you make it simple for site visitors to contact you, ask questions or purchase? Think about these questions!

Forgotten Offline Conversion Art

Too many people do a great job online and get phone calls through their websites? And yet when prospects call, the receptionist who answers the phone is rude or uneducated or worse, too busy to chat with friends online! Or you lose prospects when they enter your dirty office, totally unorganized with files and Pizza boxes everywhere. I used to bring an attorney tons of phone calls for his services but he barely could close the deal on even 1% of the calls! You MUST learn the forgotten art of offline conversion!

Online Marketing

Search Engine Optimization

This is cool! You seat back and relax and people who search for your products or services find you on the top section of the top page of Google search results! How cool is that? The reality is different. You will NOT be on top page unless you have done all the right things with major focus on a great website that offers great content to targeted audience based on keywords.

If you are a local dentist in Baltimore you must invest on daily or weekly great educational articles about dental health to be added to your site and blog. Google rewards those who truly provide value to their site visitors instead of just sales, sales and more sales pitch! How to be on the top page of Google? Be awesome customer-centric value provider! And do NOT forget local SEO based on things such as Google Maps or Yelp, etc.

Back-links Traffic

You can get great traffic from back links from other sites. Write a great educational article for your local paper and if they publish it on their online news section with link to your website, you will get visitors from the publisher site. Try to have other sites create a link to your site. How? Provide value for their site and their customers and audience!

Keywords-based Ads

Google Adwords is a good example of keyword-based ads. You create pay per click ads on Google and if someone searches for some keywords that you chose (e.g. San Diego Doctor) they will see your ad and be sent to your site landing page! Just test this and make sure that for every $1 you invest in ads you make $2 or more! Some people lose money in this area. DO THE TESTING FIRST and make necessary changes before you spend too much money!

Demographic-based Ads

Demographic and psychographic-based ads are like Facebook ads. You don't choose keywords but profiles such as female in certain city that likes Yoga! Facebook knows almost EVERYTHING about people these days and they use that for profiling targets of these ads. Try them and test them first.

Video Marketing

Humans are visual. You can influence through pictures, videos, sound and other modalities. Through videos, we can use sound and images to influence prospects. It is next best thing to being in front of prospects. And you can use YouTube to distribute these videos worldwide. But you r video should be high quality and relevant to go viral! But even without it, a simple intro video on your site home page can establish rapport with site visitors. But for God's sake, be your own spokes-model if you are good! Otherwise hire a spokes-model to do it for you!

Viral Marketing

You create a simple video about your cat doing something funny in from of the big monitor that happens to show your website or logo or products! And the video goes viral due to the funny cat and yet millions of people will see your logo! Do you get the idea? Focus on humor, sensual stuff, rock and roll, animals or whatever turns people on! My best tool is my Persian cat. He gets so much attention and I link that attention to my business!

Social Media Marketing

Go social young wo(man). Make thousands of friends and followers online and every time you post a message some of them will see it! Start with Facebook, Twitter, LinkedIn, Instagram, Pinterest and YouTube! Don't annoy people with your business sales pitch! Give value, be funny, reciprocate and post a business message only 10% of the time. AGAIN, don't annoy people with 10 business messages an hour! You will lose virtual friends and/or they will pay no attention to you! Get personal, caring and focus on give and take messages. Engage people, admit mistakes, and build relationships. BUILD RELATIONSHIPS, GOT IT? ☺

Affiliate Marketing

Do you have a product but want others to market it for you? Do you have a good network but have no product to sell? Affiliate marketing, within, minutes, give you what you lack!

You can sell great products of others (a percentage goes to you) or have internet marketers sell your products for you (a percentage goes to them). To get started, check CLICK BANK and COMMISSION JUNCTION (Google them)!

Email Marketing

The money is in the list! You have a list of 10000 prospects (you build it or you leased it). Now you email them about your products and services. It works! But follow the law and the Federal Trade Commission guidelines. With a push of a button 10000 people (in theory) will see your marketing email. Are you capturing emails when people visit your website by offering them an incentive to give you their emails?

Article Marketing

Write great articles (that educates your business prospects) and distribute them to high quality article distribution sites. The idea is to provide value to prospects so they would come to you when the need an expert in the field. A good example is http://ezinearticles.com/?expert=Koz_Khosravani

Press release Distribution

Sending out hundreds of louse press releases worked quite well with search engines during the Jurassic era! These days you don't get real search engine benefits. So the press release should be AWESOME so real news media personalities would contact you and interview you about an aspect of your business that can truly help the news media audience. And yes you might even get some traffic from back links if the news media online site refers to you and your website. But the REAL value is to get publicity. It does wonder for some of my clients like Day Spa, Museums and other entities.

Joint Venture (JV) Marketing

Why go after prospects one at a time (and build relations with them that might take months or years) if you can find Joint Venture partners who already have relations with tens of thousands of your prospects? If you can provide value to their list, you might be able to get great exposure. Not only the JV partner can introduce your services to tens of thousands if their network but they already have relations with their network so when they introduce you to them, they are endorsing you as well! One of the best marketing methods – Other People's Network (OPN)...

Online Media Appearance

Try to get on a local radio or TV show as a guest. It will be a great publicity for you. But you must offer something of the value to their viewers or listeners. Be creative when you approach them.

Blog Marketing

Write great blog posts that educate your audience. Build a group of followers of your blog and in a long term you can turn many of these followers into clients and customers.

Offline Marketing

Business Networking

Go to local Meetup groups or the local city chamber of commerce meetings. In the age of internet, there are still great marketing opportunities through one and one meetings in networking events.

Media Ads

These days, thanks to competition from the internet, you can purchase super cheap ads on local radio and TV channels. If you sell stuff to the local audience, this can work quite well for you.

Media Appearance

It is not easy to be a guest on Oprah show or similar shows. And yet, if you can get yourself invited, it will do wonders for your business. Study the show's past guests and what they offered. That might help you with your approach.

Public Relations

When you have enough money, and if relevant, hire a PR firm to help your business marketing. It works for many companies. But for a small business start-up, I recommend doing other stuff shown you in this book. You can even do do-it-yourself PR...

Direct Marketing

In some cases, I have sent post cards, mails and even hanged flyers in people's doors! For some firms, this old fashioned direct marketing technique still works. My dentist client printed and had people distribute 5000 flyers in his neighborhood. He made lots of money based on very small marketing budget, using direct marketing approach. It works for some businesses...

Tele-Marketing

I hate telemarketing calls but they work. Just follow the law. Hire a good tele-marketing firm (many good ones I found in Utah for whatever reason), make sure you have permission to call people (always pay attention and follow the no-calls directory) and never annoy people. Do it right and legal and this method of marketing can work for you...

Hosting Events

I have made lots of money hosting networking and business events. I initiate the events and made money through the door fee, sponsor fee and even took a percentage of the sales from other famous speakers I hired to speak in front of 'my' people! This can be a goldmine if done right. Look into it. You can become a local business celebrity. I hosted my own branded events; hosted TEDx events and helped others in other cities to host their events. It is very exciting and fulfilling but lots of work. Do it small with a small meeting of

10 people; make your mistakes in small events; and then go to higher level events.

Public Speaking

I have spoken in my own events as well as in other people's events (audiences as large as 14,000). It is amazing how it gives you credibility to be up there behind the podium. I gained many clients who at some point heard me in some event. If you can't get invited to speak in other people's events, organize your own event and make yourself one of the speakers.

Door-to-Door Marketing

Yes it works. My buddy provides home networking and computer/network solutions. He placed flyers on 1000 apartments near where he lived. He got 4 clients. They became his clients for years every time they needed virus protection stuff, adding a wireless printer, etc. You get the picture. But don't annoy people and follow the law and the complex rules.

Circle of Peers Networking

Mastermind Groups

See explanation under the "Success Education" section.

Becoming a Celebrity

Yes with the ease and low cost of video production and editing, you can create your own online shows. Be the start of your own show. If you are a dentist, create weekly shows about dental health and distribute it online. The sky is the limit. Hire a spokes-model to interview you about your field or industry. Use video green screen (chroma-keying) technology to place yourself and your spokes-model in a virtual news room... So many possibilities these days to be a virtual celebrity! It can turn into $$$$

Neuro-Marketing

See explanation under the "Success Education" section.

Mobile Marketing

Mobile Sites

As of now more people use their mobile phones to view your website than using their laptops or desktops! So is your site mobile friendly? You have 2 choices: make your site mobile friendly or build a 2nd site as mobile site and have your main site transfer people who are using mobile devices away from your main site into your mobile site. In effect, you have 2 sites for your business. I prefer using 1 site but making it mobile friendly. These days, even your search engine rankings on Google can suffer if your site is not mobile friendly.

Mobile Apps

Beside your mobile site, you can own a mobile app. People can download it from their iTunes or Google Play store and install it on their mobile phones. But it must be useful. For example, for my online banking, I installed Bank of America mobile app and use that to do all my online banking. Mobile apps are like good old software applications for desktops but in small version suited to small storage and memory capabilities of mobile devices. For business marketing, create something useful that can be truly valuable for your prospects.

SMS/MMS Marketing

Just like sending marketing mass mail or mass email, you can send mass text messages (both SMS and multimedia-based MMS) to thousands of people with a push of a button! But just like the above methods, you need to follow the law and perform permission-based SMS/MMS marketing. In plain English, you must have permission from the owners of these phone numbers to send them text messages. Don't send too many and don't annoy people.

QR (Quick Response) Marketing

With QR (Google it) code, you can get audience's attention and target them with optimized targeted marketing. They are like bar codes but can contain much more data about your business. Your prospects can even download your business marketing information by scanning your QR code using their mobile phone (with a right app).

Location-based Marketing

With mobile phones you can target prospects in even small geographic area (e.g. your favorite mall). The technology changes so fast and yet I think this is the wave of future. Look into it.

Sales Automation

CRM Tools

Comprehensive CRM (customer relationship management), tools allow you to integrate many operational and marketing features of your business using an enterprise-level software. The CRM software is a term used to describe a large category of enterprise or business-class software that covers a broad set of software to help your firm manage customer & prospect data, customer interaction, automate sales, marketing and customer support. You need this for later stage of your business. Start with the following tools first even though most CRM tools contain the following tools.

Email/News Blasters

Services such as aweber or verticalresponse allow you to grab customer data in pre-designed form, and use the service to market your services to these people by email, newsletters, etc. You NEED this tool in order to build a great prospect list for your business.

Lead Pages

This is a very specialized landing page that is designed to get prospect leads for you. Check out leadpages.net for such service. I highly recommend such services for a newbie.

Autoresponders

This is great software that allows you to send pre-arranged messages to your clients and prospects. For example, after you gained someone's email address, you can program your software so it send them weekly (or any date in future) marketing or educational emails.

Automated Apps & Plug-ins

Many website builders and other software or online services offer plug-ins that can enhance your online presence, your online marketing and more. These are extensions to your existing sites to make them do more real easy.

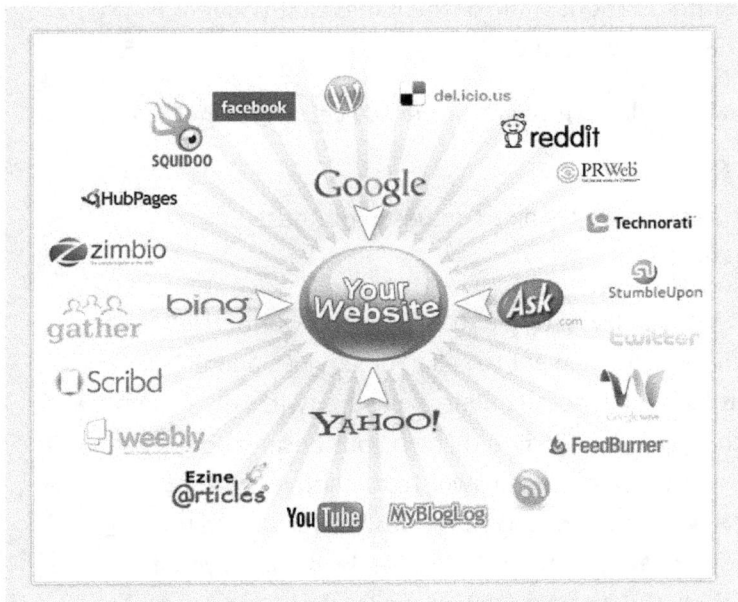

Strategies For Implementation

Ok you are now exposed to roughly 51 issues related to your business success and marketing. What you need to do now is to educate yourself about some of the issues that you feel are appropriate for your needs.

However, I would like to give you some advice about where to start.

Decide on what you are trying to do based on these important issues:

Your Goals: What are you trying to do? Do you want to sell products online? Do you want to sell your services online? Or do you want to just get some online exposure (without selling anything) that can indirectly help your business or whatever you are doing? The answer to the above questions will show you which one of the 51 shades is appropriate for you and under what conditions. For example, it shows you if you need a powerful website (selling services) vs. an e-commerce site (selling products) vs. just a simple mini site (getting publicity).

Where you are: For a total newbie super small business, all you need is a simple website to get started. But if you are opening a large dental practice in major US city, you might need a large website, and external blog and even other forms of online presence. For a small size newbie, you can do free social media marketing whereas the dental practice might want to go beyond social media and spend good amount of money on pay per click (PPC) advertising, seeking a PR firm, etc.

Your budget: Like the previous example, certain business should definitely invest in PPC advertising (not to mention many other marketing tasks) while a small business with no budget should use their free time to gain exposure on social media and even on search engines.

Now, I want to give you more in-depth information about some of the marketing and branding issues that I hope will help you further. Here we go!

Online Reputation Management For Corporations

Today if you apply for a job, there are very few instances where interviewers ask for references - they simply turn to Google to get the answers they need. The Internet has become part of people's daily existence, and it is the most revolutionary medium for communication ever experienced. Individuals and businesses are using the Internet for information and communication and nothing holds them back to vent their feelings for the world to see.

No longer is corporate online reputation management only associated with big brands. Even individuals and small businesses are targeted with venomous comment that can put them out of business permanently. There was a time before the Internet came about, when complaining about services or products was never done publicly. Not only that, companies didn't engage with their customers the way they do today and customers played a passive role too, never daring to voice their feelings in a powerful way. Bad publicity and putting a company or brand in the limelight for all the wrong reasons has become commonplace and can spell disaster for a business.

Corporate online reputation management services are becoming highly sought after in order to help businesses maintain a positive on-line presence.

Today anyone can say anything about anybody online. Social media has meant that consumers can have an enormous audience with whom they can vent their anger and share all their grievances with. Consumers are passing comments about you and your brand via different online platforms. These platforms are:

- blogs and forums

- social networking sites such as LinkedIn, Facebook and Twitter

- review sites

- information and resource sharing sites

There are actually very few laws in place to regulate what is posted online. It is mind boggling to contemplate that Yelp, which is a leading ratings and review site is visited by no less than 40 million consumers during the month, and that customers are looking at some 14 million submitted reviews.

Imagine the extent of the damage done to your company if a disgruntled employee (or even an anonymous competitor) had to place negative images or comments on this particular review site?

Just one negative review can dissuade many future would-be prospects from ever being interested in your products or services.

Improving Your Online Reputation

There are many firms and that offer online reputation management services. Some firms offer an excellent array of services and some, well, don't.

If you need online reputation management (ORM) assistance, you must focus on a few things to protect yourself and to get good results.

Always try to treat others right and avoid any online reputation issues. It is much easier to apologize once (especially if warranted) than spend hundreds of hours and thousands of dollars fighting an online attack.

Never get angry and try to attack the attacker! It will make things worse. Sometimes a 3rd party such as an ORM firm can mediate between the 2 parties, and get great results with minimal cost.

Always use various online tools (e.g. Google alerts) to monitor the cyberspace to see what is being said about you. The sooner you find out about and online attack, the easier to deal with the issue.

Claim your virtual real estate. You must, sooner or later, claim various online entities that exist about you and your firm! Believe or not, many sites, blogs, social and review profiles exists about you that you can claim (local business listing) or build yourself (mini sites and blogs)

When you try to choose an online reputation management firm to hire, check their own reputation and the reputation of the firm staff. Ask for references and engage them in an in-depth interview to see exactly what they will do for you. Have everything and I mean everything in writing, on the contract.

Never accept the claim that the ORM firms cannot guarantee results. If they have years of experience in the field, they can guess the results and take some of the risk. The contract must state the guarantees and warranties.

Reverse engineer the ORM process: In plain English, see the Google search results for people or firms similar to yours and see what shows up about them. If for example, they have a listing on meetup.com and shows on the top page, you might want to have a Meetup about your favorite topic too with proper keywords.

Finally, some ORM techniques could involve the use of the law and attorneys. Make sure the ORM firm you want to hire has excellent relations with a law firm that specializes in an online reputation defense. We do! It is a combined power of the law and the knowledge of technology that can get clients the best results.

Web Design Warning!

Most people of course hire web designers to build a website! The problem of course is that you don't want just a website. Instead you want customers and clients for your business. Hence, the website should be build with marketing goals in mind. If your web designer has no experience in online marketing or search engine optimization, then they will build you a virtual equivalent of a resort but forget to build virtual roads to lead to that resort!

In plain English, no customers will visit your resort if there are no roads leading to it from nearby towns! What good that resort will do for you? Bankruptcy!!

So make sure you hire a web designer who either knows SEO and online marketing, or works in cooperation with such professionals. Too many clients want fancy sites but can't understand that the site must have SEO components in it such as SEO tags, SEO-based content, back links from legitimate (kosher) sources and more.

So, please make sure that whoever you hire to build a website for your business views the images in this book to get a feel on the synergy between the website and online marketing (e.g. how web design and structure should have SEO in mind while delivering great content to site visitors)!

Do-It-Yourself Web Design Issues

When it comes to professionally designing a website, you have to be sure to have your priorities ahead of you. For instance, you would not focus on making a website geared towards musicians with design that is geared towards conservative lawyers – two different audiences!

You have to be sure to have a target audience as well as a bunch of other elements all come together. There are services that can help you with that out of Orange County, California where our website design firm can bring the most out of your ideas and site.

The first thing to remember is to focus on quality. There is no rush to a perfect website and you have to be sure that quality vastly outweighs quantity. You have to be sure that your website has a target market and it is geared towards the people you want visiting your website. The goal of any website is to be a great marketing tool and that it represents whatever brand you are pushing.

Once you are able to put that creativity to good use, you will see amazing traffic potential. Another element to take into account is to not have it too busy with too much content. What this means is to not overcrowd your website with a bunch of inane details and situations that just do not matter.

Less truly is more when it comes to most websites and it would behoove you to really understand that concept.

Also, remember that, along with the less is more mantra, that a few seconds can really make all the difference in your website. Today's generation does not have the same attention span we all had when we were younger...

If someone goes to your site, they will usually know if the site is worth their time within the first minute or so of viewing. If you have too much on your site, not enough appeal, and it does not catch their attention, they will not take the time to view what you have to offer.

Of course, in some cases, if you have decades of experience and content, and for certain audiences, you could have a busy site...

The last couple of elements to remember are that you need to attract a larger audience and remember the programming language you want to use to develop your website. Attracting a larger audience can mean finding the perfect website design firm that specializes in search engine optimization and other elements, and picking current trends to attract them even more.

Also, be sure to know the programming language and all the elements that make it up. You see, web design by web designers will not get you traffic and customers!

Instead, you need to hire internet marketers to design your website. Internet marketers know how to add search engine-related tags and elements to your site to rank well on Google.

Designing your website starts from the mind and computer and once you realize that, the possibilities of your site can be endless.

I recommend that you build your own website with free available online services (e.g. sites.google.com) even if you want to hire others. Why? By building your own site, you will get a feel for what is going on, therefore, you can communicate better with web designers that you hire.

Local Marketing

Listen, if you have a local business that offers services to audiences within the 20 miles ratio of your location, you must pay attention to local marketing.

Always start with Google Maps. Make sure you are listed on Google Maps. These days you can get on Google for free and gain great amount of publicity. How?

Visit https://www.google.com/business and follow the guidelines and steps. In no time, you will be on Google Maps and search results.

One tip: Try to add as much information about your business as possible. These include text, images, videos, etc. Make sure you write the address, phone, email, website address and other relevant information correctly.

Then move on to Yahoo and other local search engines and directories. These include City Search, Yelp, Bing, Yahoo and many others. You can even use a paid service from Yahoo that submits your site to 50+ local directories at once. It cost a little money ($29.95 as of the time of this writing) but you save a lot of time and get massive local exposure. To see if their service is good for you, visit: https://smallbusiness.yahoo.com/local-listings

THANK YOU FOR READING! NOW IT IS TIME TO TAKE ACTION. PLEASE UNDERSTAND THAT GETTING EDUCATED IS JUST THE BEGINNING. YOU MUST TAKE ACTION AND IMPLEMENT WHAT YOU LEARNED.

THIS BOOK WAS WRITTEN FOR TOTAL BEGINNERS TO THE FIELD OF APPLIED MARKETING. WE HOPE IT OPENED YOUR EYES ABOUT MANY AREAS THAT YOU SHOULD LEARN MORE ABOUT. GOOD LUCK...

About the Author

http://www.KozWealthSystems.com

Koz Khosravani is an Internet expert, a Computer Information Systems consultant, an Information Technology and educational technology lecturer, and Teaching Fellow at various colleges and universities, including Harvard University, UC-Irvine, UC-San Diego, and UCLA Extension Schools.

Koz is a national speaker who has shared the stage with The President of the United States, Donald Trump, Tony Robbins,

George Foreman, Lisa Nichols, David Bach, Chris Howard and many other top speakers.

Koz is the only Internet Expert who was invited to be on stage with Donald Trump, Tony Robbins, and others to speak at major wealth Expos in New York and Chicago Convention Centers.

He has been active in the field of Information Technology and education for approximately fifteen years as a software engineer, project manager, educator, trainer, and consultant. He has trained technical employees at various Fortune 500 companies, including Digital Equipment Corporation, Raytheon, Hughes, Edison International, and Boeing (M-Douglas).

His area of specialization includes Internet promotion and marketing, Internet conversions (converting site visitors to buyers and repeat buyers), digital movie editing, digital movie production and post-production, educational technology, e-business security & back-end integration, distributed relational database management systems, wireless technologies, networking, web development, and distributed applications.

Koz designed boot-camp-type fast-track Web Mastering programs for both UCLA and UC-Irvine to benefit those who want to learn about all aspects of website design, construction, and implementation - all in one intense week.

Koz taught a variety of Educational and Instructional Technology courses, including the Internet for Educators, Online Research for Educators, and Advanced Microcomputers in the Classroom (Clear Credential).

He designed and deployed a variety of short business workshops and consulting sessions in the areas of negotiations, communications, business management, MIS, and investments. In addition, he has served on the UCI and UCLA Extension School's advisory committees to develop certificate programs in E-Business and Educational Technology.

Koz created a new program at UCI Extension (2000-2001) entitled "E-Commerce for Entrepreneurs & Small Business Owners". He also taught E-Business Technology overview, E-Business Back-end Integration, and E-Business Security for UCI's Business division. On a lower "system" level, Koz taught VAX-Macro systems programming and Macro-11 at Harvard University.

He has served on the UCLA Alumni Association Board of Directors, UCLA Wooden Athletic Center Board of Governors, UCLA's Executive Vice Chancellor's Academic Planning & Budget Advisory Committee (APBAC), UCLA Academic Senate's Professional School's Restructuring Committees, and UCSA Board of Governors, as well as other educational and social organization's governing boards.